Singing Underwater

Susan Wicks grew up in Kent and studied French at the Universities of Hull and Sussex, where she wrote a D. Phil. thesis on the fiction of André Gide. She has taught in France and at University College, Dublin. She now lives with her husband and two daughters in Tunbridge Wells, and works as a part-time tutor for the University of Kent.

SUSAN WICKS

Singing Underwater

faber and faber

LONDON · BOSTON

First published in 1992
by Faber and Faber Limited
3 Queen Square London WC1N 3AU

Phototypeset by Wilmaset Ltd, Wirral
Printed in Great Britain by
Clays Ltd, St Ives plc

© Susan Wicks, 1992

Susan Wicks is hereby identified as the author of
this work in accordance with Section 77 of the
Copyright, Designs and Patents Act, 1988

A CIP record of this book is available from the British Library

ISBN 0 571 16724 1

To my father,
in memory of my mother

Acknowledgements

Poems from this collection have appeared in *Ambit*, *Iron*, *London Magazine*, *The North*, *Oxford Poetry*, *Poetry Durham*, *Poetry East* (USA), *Poetry Nottingham*, *Poetry Review*, *Poetry Wales* and *The Rialto*.

Contents

I

On Turning Away

I touch you and feel myself
touched, speak to you and hear
a child's voice speaking.
Your fingers at my neck
part my wet flesh,
support me, wobble-headed
in a bath of warm water
stained familiar with rust.
I suck at you
feeling a finger
knead the escaping nipple,
stroke my mouth into focus.
I crawl through your
concertina of muscle,
hear my first breath
stopped, drawn inwards.
I float, curled,
my limb-buds re-folding,
the precious membranes
re-forming. Divided cells
knit again simply.
A speck clings to blood-
cushioned walls.

Oh let me turn away
from you, hide my vacant body
in a blanket. I am
too tired now to learn
how babies begin.

After Sixteen Years

You sprawl from the bed
to the floor, a sweet ache
of space between limbs, no
words. I curl, sniffing you,
feel the brush of strange hair
against my knees. Pictures
are thrown up on screens:
our old wallpaper, a milk-float
in a lane, a woman
buying pastries, a tree.
You see gangsters, islands,
black satin, chalk-dust. I
comfort the tip of your lost tongue.

Sometimes we still do it
in our sleep.

On an Error in Your Passport

You were born unexpectedly
exactly a year too early,
making us parents while we slept.

He and I need not have known
each other. You were unwanted,
unthought of, unscanned,

unprepared for. A day and night
of panic was all we had.
I lay shaking on a bed.

You were our first emergency.
The screen across my belly
seemed makeshift. I cried

Do it, oh do it. From the dark,
raking with cold fingers,
they lifted you free

and dangled you high over
me like a garden carrot,
your long head orange as if in sun —

and he, by a fluke of timing
not there, not having come.

Four months later the sickness began.

Singing Underwater

(to my daughter on her birthday)

Together we go down,
knees bent to our chins,
hands fanning the water.
We crouch on the bottom
shivered with reflections,
where thrashing limbs live,
and white-boned feet.
Your hair escapes outwards,
teased by sudden currents.
Your gold eyeballs protrude.
You tug on me and gesture,
mouth opening and closing,
wrapping me in new water
from my crown to my cold toes.
In a rush of blind bubbles
your underwater raspberry
bursts the surface with a roar.
But underneath, the thin tone
of the newborn, lamb, kitten,
or monster. Happy Birthday.
I recognize your tune.

It is not difficult,
the repertoire of the fishes.
You rise with me from three feet
of water, and you splutter.

On the Lake

My daughter walks on water.
Quick blades beating, she scuds
across blue distance, gold
anorak plumped by the wind.
Then, flat on her back, she laughs
at the sky, the horizon, the water
under her shot with bubbles.

Now I am just good enough
to pass over her, bend
my stiff arms into wings, scoop
her from the frozen surface.
Our old skates jump grooves, powder
loose ice-fragments, carry us
from one shore to the other.

Nose-bleed

White figure hunched on the stairs,
you breathe blood into clenched fingers,
dyeing handkerchief, carpet, pillow,
bedspread: small animal shot
on snow. You blink and shiver,
pinch back the rich stream
as they taught you. Gently
I wipe blood-crust from furrows,
hold my own breath, counting.

Now the whites lie soaking
in salt; the bed is stripped.
On my knees I track blood spots,
rubbing at your dark coinage
to make this stubborn floor shine.

Voices

My mother's voice, long-distance,
is thin, the silence of sea-beds
in it, darkness, the weight of water.
From a room upstairs my sick child
calls, and I go to her: high
shapes of wind-lifted branches
ripple across her bedspread.
This one I can comfort, her body
plump as grapes, her light hair
breathable: read her the old stories
in a gamut of assumed voices. All day
I run up and down the bare treads,
listen for signals, for a long space
of silence, carry messages or snacks
or empty plates in both directions.

Let Me Dance

Let me dance myself larger.
Let me dance myself into the trees
swaying to the tip of my little finger,
grass swishing between my knees.

Let me dance myself enormous,
feet flapping, breasts like great bags,
a belly that wobbles houses.
Let me trample the fields to rags.

And then I can dance with my children,
my little one clinging to my neck,
my big one's feet covering my feet,
and room for one more on my back.

Snow Monkeys

We saw a programme about snow monkeys
and marvelled at how the old mother,
paralysed below the waist, still cared
for her children, how through the winter
she still dragged herself and slithered
in a clot of snow to a lip of summer
by hot springs; how she went on
to have more children as her daughters
matured around her, still groomed them
with stiff fingers, snowflakes in her
beard, the folds of skin still hanging
from her eyes intelligently.

First Words

My father in a trilby still travels
to Lincoln's Inn, his baby daughter
held up to smell sun on the flowers,
da-da-ing to passing trains.

My mother laments her old doll,
clipped spiky and ludicrous;
still turns slow somersaults on poles,
screaming herself beyond the bank of words.

My daughters have lovers already,
crumpled under pillows, or folded,
surviving the wash in pockets,
illegible as leaves.

My children have journeys, cancer, childbirth,
scribbled on their wrists in felt tip.

Amish Friendship Bread

Day one: do nothing. Accept
what has been given
in a blue and white bowl.

Day two: stir. Bubbles
rise to the surface. The morning
is cool, the window open.
A sparrow scatters drops from
wings dipped in my birdbath.

Day three: stir.
The mixture smells yeasty,
foams like a new planet.
My spoon turns and turns it,
folds it on itself in live
furrows. The sun moves. Children
call across from treehouses.

Day four: stir. It is
puffed and pale as a face.
My spoon punctures it
with sighs. To the east
clouds funnel the darkness,
tornadoes level barns,
trees whip the air smooth again.

Day five: add milk,
measured in a cup. Add flour
and sugar. In its bowl
the batter seethes, crusting
to unexpected proportions.
My daughters, home from school,
crash the house door open,
throw down their backpacks,
catch me heady at the last scraping.

Day six: now there is more
surface for the spoon's wake
to disappear in, a wider
noose of stirring. Through mist
I hear the long flat hoot
of a goods train at a crossing.
Later, sun streaks my knuckles.

Day seven: it swells again,
leaves a sticky tide-mark on
Pyrex. At midnight
I turn off the strip-light
and think I still see it,
the pale rise of moon-cheeks,
twin nostrils black as holes.
I stand at the screen-door
listening for the cry of owls.

Day eight: as I pass through
I write my name with a knife blade.
The reek of yeast
follows me upstairs,
outside, clings to me, heavy
as a child swinging from my neck.

Day nine: I have beaten it
more than once. Now you and I
lie bloated as two babies.
My knees curl in to your belly,
your mouth still drags at the nipple.
Words cream in us as the house
cracks to our combined breathing.

From the hot kitchen
the smell reaches me. I stretch
myself in sun, turn, close my eyes,
my hungry children inoffensive as bees.
Day ten: the bread is ready.

Give
a cup of the culture
to each of three friends,
or to your daughters,
in a small container.

Tell them this is day one.

Mermaid

My daughter lies in her bath,
a mermaid in two inches.
As the water slurps and gurgles,
she giggles, sealed tight
into her tail, half-beached,
small fronds of pubic hair
combed parallel like so much
emerald weed.

Shall I go now, shall I
leave her to her two inches
of ripples, long legs
forming like a woman's,
scallop of breasts, wet hair
flopping? But she slaps
her fish-tail on the bottom
and still wants me.

One day soon she will
demand a closed bathroom,
soaping her woman's body
in silence, or quietly singing
and not call me
when she stands to step over
the side of the bath gracefully
as a dancer taking a knife-edge.

II

Head-lice

They told me, always keep a bottle,
labelled, on the top shelf,
for the unwelcome discovery.
Then one day I found them,
pearls in the undergrowth.
I could have held them in my hand.
But murder is a modest little need
you can prepare for, like love,
or contraception of various descriptions.

Child

Would you like to hang my baby from a hook
head downwards, like a bunch of dried flowers?
Caress the silk wood of the coffin
and say Yes, it was a good tree
a good angle to cut it
a tree you might lie under in your old clothes
and dream?

Would you like to catch my child between your hands,
rock it to sleep as if it were born already
sitting on a strange bed in the darkness
remember life between contracted phrases
like a long gasp in silence
thinking Yes, it was a good way to listen
a good way to hear yourself breathing
an instrument found in an attic and played on
big with old tunes?

Would you like to hold it with me
folded in the hollow of our bodies like a bird
feel the blind mouth searching
taking your nipple for mine in the small warm hours
and say Yes, it is a good night
broken by hunger broken by crying
not much sleep but shadows bulging on the ceiling
a night you will remember in times of mourning
and start to sing?

No Strings

Would you mind if I were to do it
ever so gently?
Would it be unacceptable?
I could eat them one by one slowly
like sweeties.
No one need ever know
there was a man in the car.

Or slide it wet across my skin
up under the armpit
until it drew blood in secret.
No one need ever suspect
I was not alone.

Or again, I could tighten the string
round my wrist, round my finger,
until the dead flesh dropped away.

Moderato

(*after Marguerite Duras*)

My child never played the piano.
It was the clarinet mostly.
You can't count a recorder.
And no escaping boat crossed the window
from frame to horizon.
She played in a pink-gold room under the lamp,
and the flowered curtains remained closed.

There was no murder in a French café.
No crowd gathered.
Our crimes were quite bloodless.
No one was escorted to the closed van,
desire still smeared on their faces.
For us it took somewhat longer than a week.

But there was a magnolia tree, certainly.
The smell of flowers was all down the hill.
I didn't actually press them to my bosom.
My bosom isn't of that sort.
But I did have one in my pocket for a while,
pink and white with brown edges.
And if you had offered me a knife
I'd have slit my throat gladly,
and you might have tried dipping your fastidious
prick briefly in the hole.

Ha Ha Bonk

Love the Big Bad joke for adults,
electric custard, gooseberry in a lift.
Why couldn't he have come up with something better?
Knock, knock, I got tired of asking.
Irish stew in the Name of the Law.

And why did the Burglar saw the legs off his bed?
So we could hear the springs creak more clearly?
I wanted to lie low too. Very low, lying with you.
Lying all the time if I could.
Was it that I had stolen something?

And now it goes Ha ha bonk
all down the passage.
A Man laughing his head off.
If I see it rolling I shall pick it up,
carry its belly-laugh with me on a silver plate.

Poacher

He seemed almost to like animals.
He stroked their muzzles sometimes.
He was a kind man.
And he gave them no promises:
when the trap's teeth snapped shut,
their own light feet had triggered the spring.

There was no dishonesty in that, surely?
He wore a dark jersey in the dark,
only his hands white in the moonlight.
He did what he had come for.
What did you expect to run into,
stretched low as a shadow under the black trees?

And his bag was there to receive you
merely for discretion's sake along the moonlit path.
He only did what they all do,
except that he would use his voice sometimes
to coax the wildest ones forwards
on to the wire with a soft laugh.

Snap

It was an amateurish angle
for a photograph, heavy trees
reaching, spire's silver needle,
wet grass falling away
beyond a paling. But there was also
the dark, and I had no camera.

Still, I took a snap of your wrist
by feel, my fingers crawling
across dry skin to take
a sliver of flesh in moonlight,
handless, armless – a section
just thick enough for an expert
to tell which way the hairs grew.

Out of the Zoo

We exchanged words
as people do who meet
in anonymous places,
the netting overhead
starred with trapped peanuts.

As you got up to go
a mouse ran out
of the folds of your trousers,
let itself be caught, its frantic
fear-pulse slowed in my bed of fingers
till it lay curled and quiet.

As you opened the door
lice pattered on the pages of my book.
I wrapped them in pocket-fluff,
put them to sleep in the darkness
between my breasts, to fuse
and spread there like milk-drops.

When you left the train
there was a worm on the seat,
wrinkled as an old nametape.
I wound him in a skein,
and made him a nest
in the soft tissue
under my tongue.

Your bland voice however
refuses to be captured.

Rebeck

This is your rebeck,
a swelling shape, all female,
polished by searching fingers
yet unfinished, smooth as skin
yet soundless, corpse in a forest
clearing, flesh of the dead tree.

This is your rebeck,
half made, half dreamed. Your searching
fingers play across the wood. The curves
glisten and swell, all female
body bloated with silence:
no scratch or scrape
of sound to shudder the darkness;
only the night and breath enough
to make a dead twig laugh.

Give me your rebeck
and I will smash its satin
ribs in half and hang
the empty belly in my garden
from a green branch.
Birds will crust it with their droppings,
puncture it at daybreak
with instinctive singing.

Anonymous

Six days it took me to do it,
the sweat running off my fingers,
every copy a new masterpiece,
reshaping your smooth world.
I made them all, collage of paper
clippings trembling on the carpet
like coiled moons,
gum worming its necklace,
the mother-segments of sliced sounds.

They were their own sentences,
cut and pasted together,
delighting the fraud squad
who visited you on the seventh day.

Second Coming

You came to us in two colours,
hair and coat streaming,
your lips pursed on echoes.
Your offer was unrepeatable.

You did as we asked you,
gold instrument glinting:
you rid us of our children,
piped them away cleanly.

The last time I saw them
they crouched in the cave-mouth
in a glow of yellow half-life
washed by a dark flood.

Now a grey tide surrounds us,
crush of snouts and bellies
coursing in buried conduits,
succulent as fat fish.

Will you come and take them,
pipe us free of vermin,
our parti-coloured Saviour,
god in two parts?

We sit in our closed houses,
tight and childless as children,
waiting for your second coming,
guarding our precious rats.

Swing-bin

Furled white plastic,
last limp flag on a roll,
this bin-liner (swing, not pedal)
was painlessly separated
along the perforations provided.

Its sides swell now with peelings.
Tea-bags wilt into crannies.
Crumbs of seed-cake dust
the surface with stale pollen
(my mother's tested recipe).

A roll-on deodorant
nudges old rags aside; torn
envelopes, a twist of string
(the kind my father used
to make us kites as children).

Litter of garlic-husk
confetti (to please my husband
once a week on Fridays);
your tapes: rich swill of
Beethoven, Monteverdi,
Katja Kabanova; spaghetti maggots
slide with the subterranean
tremor of springing leaves.

Toad Rock

I knew a man who had a creature
smooth and featureless as you.
He gave it to his wife.
It crouched on the hearth-stone.
White fingers squirmed in the dark
under its cold belly.

It was tired, apparently;
had eaten at too many tables,
oozed on too many staircases;
distrusted the silk of sheets
between its webbed toes.

Worn smooth as sandstone,
no hand-holds, hardly a dimple,
you shrug off your scars eventually.
My initials have given birth
to a two-season tree.

But the golden ball
sits denting my pillow
where my head should be,
still dripping pondwater.

Forgetting Hallsands

*(After dredging work connected with the building
of Plymouth harbour, the village of Hallsands was
finally washed away by storms in 1917. Only one old
woman remained.)*

It might have been early morning, it might have been
    evening
when she first saw the dredgers at work out in the bay.
Perhaps the ledge of shingle shifted slightly, polished
pebbles turning to gold on that ordinary day.

She listened for signs, sensing the sea-bed crumble,
measuring time and tide-span against her hand,
but the echoes died in circles, criss-crossing,
and old waves crashed home on the old sand.

Was it a year later, was it much longer,
that the earth sank where the women used to walk?
Half the houses combed away, and half still standing,
scabby with seaweed, bladders drying on the dry stalk.

There were marks on the walls of buildings, warning the
    living;
where the shingle had reached the stones were black.
She felt the land fall, and the day turned over,
swirling at her heels, glinting, and sucked back.

It was in spring, that equinox, or was it October? –
house after house cleaned on its stone slab,
words torn from mouths in the storm's doorway,
the corner cottage lifted, lurching like a crab.

There were two storms, surely, to crack the village open,
brittle bodies powdered for the sea's bones.
She still hears, turning it over and over,
one freak tide smoothing its bed of stones.

Now, tripping on ruins, plagued by the harsh breathing
of rocks in water, shingle under the rain,
she stops to take shelter in the wells of chimneys,
scanning the dark circle for a belated sign.

III

I Am Man-made

I am man-made.
My father made me,
softened and pulled me,
thumbed me full of crescents.

I am man-made.
My teachers made me,
threw and turned me,
textured me with scratches.

I am man-made.
The Devil made me,
moistened and coiled me,
fired me, glazed me
blue-black and green.

Now they are gone,
by whom shall I be seen?

Infants

The day thou gavest
with what shall I mend it
there are holes in the roof now
to let out the singing

fragments of broken slate
now the day is over
jelly on the wibble-wobble
milk bent straws in the crate

tippity-tappity on my shoulder
smoke-stains under the eaves
they done it them two together
cowardy cry ouch custard cry

before the huntsman shoots me dead
I never I honestly never I never
windows open to the old voices
steel across the sky.

Boys' Camp

This is the boys' camp: sun
pierces the shelter of branches;
the floor is littered with sleeping-
bags, dead cans. They use
spent ring-pulls for currency,
build a fire of old comics.
Smoke seeps through a jagged hole.
Along the path a voice cries
'Halt!' and you stop breathing,
paralysed. Who goes there?
Then the arrows come, narrowly
missing your cheek, glancing
from tree-trunks into brambles,
poisoned, or heavy with paper
and rubber bands: messages shot
from the undergrowth of leaves.

Riding

This is the way the gentleman rides
the lady, trit-trot between unwrinkled sheet
of sky and the earth's soft mattress,
neat as for a gymkhana, dressage kisses
displayed on her sleek forehead.

The farmer studying the fallow
clouds one lost season, slowly
explores his valley of flattened corn.
Clip-clop, blind rider crossing the twilight
bridges, he feels his way home.

But the old man has it, his body
splayed on the ditch-bank, pumping like a
frog's, mouth slippery with leaves,
knobbed fingers still clawing at
contours. You shriek with laughter
at a face seen from underneath.
Hobble-dee, hobble-dee.

Sea-anemone

Dark bud, swollen and shining
in the long blink of the tide,
you guard your salt cavern,
sucked bare in your crack of dark weed.

You are closed now. Closed, you glisten,
fat pupil ringed with ripples.
They poke at you with driftwood,
and you are inscrutable as a cyclops.

You sit smugly under the rock
and wait for evening,
fattening yourself on silence,
gorged with sea-creatures.

You are nothing but a blind thing,
a shape, a shell, a polished stone.
A pointed stick could smash you
to a smear of moisture burnt in the sun.

But the tide will find you
with a head-dress of live serpents,
stinging the world to sleep,
licking and leaping when the eyes have gone.

Fire-stealer

He was the most silent,
cold lips cupped to the bottle.
Alone in the blank-eyed circle
he measured the darkness,
feeding his sick liver with a swig.
Then, head back, arms wide,
he amazed us, his fire grazing
the underside of rafters, his mouth
full, spurting live tongues.

Spiral Jetty

*(Created by Robert Smithson, who died searching
for a new site in 1973.)*

He was something like an artist,
using his rubble to make a jetty,
dropping his perfect spiral in the lake.

He was perfection's poor fool,
with his 292 truckloads,
making the stones sizzle for art's sake.

He was the solitary walker
over the blood-dark water
(there are things one can do from a jetty,

things one can stop oneself doing,
pacing the empty question mark and watching,
charting the rise of boulders as they bake).

Lord

Look at you lording it over us,
draped in close folds of fat,
lapped in your ample future,
as you sprinkle us your little
congregation with warm milk.

See you sit in your high chair
throwing down toys to create
a diversion, making us scuttle.

Watch you break bread,
finger-food mauled to tatters,
smeared from mouth to forehead,
daubed in murals at tray height.

Listen to you wail at night-time,
hear you yowl and whimper, pucker-faced,
as my perverse nipples rise.

Come here, let me give you a cuddle.
I can make it better.

We will rock you, we are used
to nightmares, poppet, listen,
listen to me. Child indeed.

Eve at Autun

You let them in once, the rabble
of pilgrims, craning their necks
to see stone devils, monsters,
wise men like wise monkeys
carrying stone in caskets.
Now they enter freely, no longer need
to look up to count the grapes
chiselled in clusters. Here are the
Child's legs dangling from the donkey,
here is St Joseph in his corner; almost
at eye level Judas chokes on his tongue.
This near space was an arm, a nose,
a finger. No scaffolding.
Ordinary stairs can lead to such places.
You lie on your side, thinking,
your stretched girl's body conventionally
decent. Your cheek lengthens in your hand,
the lichen of Paradise growing in your eye-
sockets, as you grope for the
one tree, now leafless,
and the door stands open, unguarded.

Rings

Let me die like an onion,
on a good block board
by a short clean knifing,
new life still at the centre,
a jet of sharp juice in the eye.
Sever me straight
before you tease me in concentric circles,
dream from dream,
twin from embryonic twinning,
sleep from waking.
Your hand is shaking.
Watch me change my shape
and shimmer under running water
if it makes you cry.

Stunt-woman

When I was born, she was the one
they lifted, her slimy crescent
of body squirming as their hands
closed on her. When hunger
nudged me, she cried, crush
of tomato-features, split skin
where her mouth was. In my mother's
arms, she rocked dangerously, grasped
with her under-sea fingers. I
shut my eyes and sucked. She
staggered, skipped, trick-skated
on hard surfaces as I still crawled,
mouthing my wants in a sour hiccup.
Always her monkey-shadow thrown
from tree-branch or diving-board or
train-roof would run before me,
the dark star of her body
a splash in the winter bushes.
And once I seemed to see her
strapped to a fast car, as if to capture
the gritty texture of distance,
her thighs cartwheeling through exhaust
as I sat with legs folded.

Later, wincing in a dark room,
I review it, scissors in hand,
asking myself who paid her,
cutting so much borrowed footage.

Hall of Mirrors

(to Mara)

In my kettle I have a long head.
My nose swells like a drop
of ripe metal, my chin is melting,
my eyes squash up to the lid.

I have a clutch of white knuckles
smooth as eggs in a steel
saucepan, hair matted with dazzle,
pores big as pin-pricks.

Crouching, I am a child sick
with mumps; as I rise
my puffed jowls puncture, my head
nods over a stainless breastplate.

On tiptoe I am pregnant again
for a moment, silver freak,
queen of the pier-palace,
my skin beaded with real water.

Post Partum

(to Mara)

When you lifted the receiver
I heard crying, my few questions
answered in raucous gasps
of need, bringing it all back
to me, soapflakes and ammonia,
nape-hair on my closed eyelids,
bars across the window.
I hear the slow creak
of wheels as I walked my daughter,
feet flapping on brick pavements
under rain, the sudden crunch
of a pothole, my own teeth
chattering. You tell me Wait
and there is a new silence
more urgent than my questions,
your mouth drooping as you unbutton
parts of yourself I can imagine.

Black and White

Old Russian woman,
arms like exposed roots,
mouth one level line of shadow,
she stands,
not noticing the petals,
not noticing the clouds,
outstaring the camera,
blossom-drift over her,
freak snowstorm in lush grass,
May-winter.

Because she is old and in black
the May-blizzard shows up on her,
freckled and full of birth as an egg.

IV

Hugo's Long-Sleeved Cardigan

was the book I read my daughter
night after night, her eyes closing
as she sucked on two fingers:
the story of a grandmother
not unlike my own mother
who counted obedient stitches
and came up with something
ill-fitting, good only for monkeys.
I can still see that cardigan
behind bars, smeared with banana,
the hairy hand emerging
from stripes, prehensile thumb
bent backwards, looped back over
trapezes, the head hanging
in confined spaces.
                    And I wish
there had been no banana,
no stripes, no monkeys'
chatter, no empty dangle
of wool, that the endless sleeves
had ended sooner, defiantly,
or that the child's arms
had inched out on needles
to meet her, a few rows longer.

Inside the Heart

(to my mother)

(*Chicago Museum of Science and Industry*)

We negotiate bloodstained spaces.
Exploring valves, we drag currents
up to the elbow. Meeting walls,
we touch muscle, ridged arteries
colder than our skin. Our feet
stumble between two chambers,
feel the glass fibre
unyielding through our thin soles.
We put out our hands to save
ourselves from falling, tumble
from the left ventricle, deaf,
dizzy with pounding. The giant
heartbeat surrounds us, faked,
larger than life,
uninterrupted.

From here your heart is small
as a bird's, its live spaces
ready to buckle in silence –
and I reeling and hammering
to get in, my body braced
like a pit-prop, my mouth
still yelling Eureka,

knowing now just where to place myself.

To You on My Birthday

On this day especially
I think of how you
felt yourself abandoned, waters
breaking in blackness as
frightened (you said) by a
horse in a field, stupidly,
you stumbled and felt me
come in a rush, leaving
you empty
four weeks too early,
being too eager (you said)
for what life had for me.
You'd smile as you told me
how Sister laughed and sat me
in the palm of her hand,
two and a bit bags
(you made it) of sugar
and said, She has everything
a young lady should have,
and you cried. (I think
those were the words exactly.)

Mother and Child

My mother's letter has been written
in pencil by a child, her own familiar
phrasing fainter, made simple, her words
losing their small footing. This is her
reception-class writing, stab and scribble
of a body's fall through darkness:
stick bones snap and settle to tinder
at the foot. *I have been silly and broken*
my arm, and I see it: my frantic father
clutches hot-water bottles, calls
999, waits at the door. Seven hours
before they can X-ray, and the break
too high for plaster. *I have been silly.*

This is my mother's first letter,
crawling to meet me across paper,
the incompetent fingers tight-bunched
as she waits for me to answer
I am so sorry, my words perfectly
aligned, so many prize pothooks.
We apologize to one another —
mother, child, grand-daughter —
slip our guilt into envelopes,
to post in the crack under the door.

Midnight Feast

(to my mother)

They suffered from strange fancies,
those waiting, ill-nourished women,
fishing for pickles with their fingers
in a night pantry, or crunching on coal,
black dust smeared on their faces.

Before my child was born I dreamed
my own birth again, the bone-petals
of my skull lapped tight
as a crocus for your impossible
small O of light, the crushed root
of me squirming white fingers,
air through my ribcage.

But you lift me and put me on you
to suck at your sweet wet wound.
I learn birth from you
by taste, indigestible as coal-lumps
or pickles, cream-thick as colostrum,

my skin stretched over child-
flesh, yet still half empty
for this, our midnight feast,
our first square meal together.

Breathing Space

He would always walk me
in dogs' mess and sweet-papers,
or out in the country
between banks of high cow-parsley,
ditches alive with nettles,
until our car in the distance
was a small box of nausea
still closed on my mother
and my skin that was cold and strange
as waxed paper, would suck in colour.
'Big breaths,' and I would breathe
perfectly as he walked me,
facing the oncoming traffic, as if
we travelled, the three of us,
under a tight lid
we could always stop to open,
wherever we were, and walk
away from, breathing deeply.

Mad Scientist

You were mad once: in mirrors
you would comb your grey hair
upwards, squint and grimace
at your horror-film reflection
to make us shriek; would lunge
dangle-armed for who knew
what reaction. I flopped,
hysterical, jelly knees
spread for the kill,
silver hiccup of bubbles
in a tankful of tubing.
You were my father, your retort
seething with tadpoles.

This morning at the mirror
I was wearing your hair.

Stilt-walker

Knowing I would never be
tall enough, my father made me
stilts, two poles to shudder
and part under me
as I swayed among branches:
my back to the wall, I practised
mounting lightly, swung into air
between cherry-blossom, fascia-boards,
fanlights; I would totter
to the corner, stick-legged,
tap out my wooden circle,
one of those clowns who
thumb their noses at gravity,
their faces shrinking into distance,
long thighs arched over small
vehicles, the bulges of ordinary feet
swaddled in cloth,
striped trousers cut for giants,
or bell-tents of skirt so wide
they might conceal fat purses
of warm rubies, a baby's wet head,
a real man crouching.

Such a Day

Sun pointed the undersides of buildings.
Trees flashed their white bones.
Brass elephants winked from glancing
windows. Your mother died.

You bought a ticket to Atlanta.
Your husband came home laughing,
Plasticine under his nails.
Your small daughter sang.

A bus turned belly-upwards,
floated to the sun's surface,
top deck half buried in a field.
Planes made white trails.

Daffodils nodded in doorways.
Your father was a scarecrow
flapping lopsided to squalls.

The dog flattened by a passing lorry
took up his skin and loped
sideways to the grass verge.

Time Zone

The clock-radio plays Albinoni
and they talk through it,
dreaming their old adagio
of closed rooms, lost children.
Mid-morning they shiver, shut
the curtain on darkness,
turn on the TV and sit
watching. Their gas hisses.
Their remaining teeth
grind on in shadow,
leave snail-paths of crumbs.
Their loose skin is gritty.
Their malted milk is cold
or swallowed by 3.30.
By 6.00 no one can reach them,
out for the count, snoring.
Just once, near bedtime,
they snort, hearing something,
half roused by a full bladder.
Is someone calling them?

Yet when the clock says sleep
they are just beginning.

Branches

I saw my father and mother standing
in a pond, against sunlight on rushes,
my mother's thin arm reaching
from between the small suns of water-lilies,
and saw that a spider
had strung threads from my father's knees
to glitter out over the water;
that their bleached bones had hardened
in the green on green of circles
and the paired blue wings of dragonflies,
the minute dance of egg-laying.
And I was glad
that they still stood there, sun-dry and reaching,
and I was grateful
that no one had needed to bury them,
shut them out of all that light.

Halfway

I

Halfway up, side on to the fall-
away staircase, silk cord dangling,
one plush slipper crushed
between banisters, an old woman
will not be moved. Head and shoulder
buttressing the numb bulk,
she braces, shudders, lets out the stopper
on a flood of warm urine, dark
fizz on worn treads; steam rises,
apricot summer and mould-scab,
fine spittle of long-bottled words.

II

Down there they keep the old
ragbag of pudding-cloths
tie-dyed in shades of skin.
Down there they stir the old
long-handled silent wishes flash
of fruit wrinkle of cold scum.
Their tongues will search you out,
probe the place you crept to hide
the pips your shrivelled babies
your fool's gold.
Bright juice to jelly strained
through a muslin scalp
your sunlit days drip overnight
from a mess of dark pulp.

III

There was a small chapel,
green wood through almond-blossom,
where the boy who pumped the organ
had his eyelids half closed.
You sang as you haven't sung since,
guiding flat clothes through the mangle,
studying the sky for weather.
Rain made mossy pools under the porch.
You sat with laced fingers, staring up
or down at his rhythmic reach and clench.

IV

Now I am at the bottom, lemon-spattered,
my camp-bed in the kitchen.
Up there my grandmother still laughs,
ravels the threads person to lost
person silk twist of voices
spider stalk-eyed in the bath;
harangues the latest invention
for two days and nights,
our old bellows jigged on her
shoulder like a fractious baby,
never drawing breath.

Michelin Lady

(D.F., in memoriam)

In the summer you were wise already.
My tortoise turned towards your garden,
straining its long string,
and fed on your lettuces.
I climbed your iron staircase
and came back with my dress
full of mixed nuts
left from some Christmas.
And in winter by the barbed firelight
I performed for you sometimes,
dressing and undressing in layers,
taking childhood off and putting on
lace from your slow collection.

Remember how I curtseyed from behind your curtain
lifting my light skirts
and tell me where it hurts.

I saw you only once this last July,
heavy as a paperweight,
your smile sliding downhill
before I could catch you.
And now you lie on a bed bloated,
your lungs full of bubbles,
not letting your friends near you
in case they should recognize the true
Michelin Lady,
while our slow car winds out
between flat fields of stubble
screened with burning.
I am coming.

Hold on tight to my finger.
Feel how the ring pulls against the knuckle's rolled skin,
and let the strongest win.